Litanies and Reiterations

Litanies and Reiterations
Dylan Kinnett

Contents

Epigraphs

"Isn't life a series of images
that change as they repeat themselves?"
— Andy Warhol

"No time for poetry but exactly what is"
— Jack Kerouac

"There is no such thing as repetition. Only insistence."
— Gertrude Stein

"to repeat, monotonously, some common word, until the
sound, by dint of frequent repetition, ceased to convey any
idea whatever to the mind"
— E.A. Poe

"Manners first, then conversation."
— Ralph Waldo Emerson

Apostrophe

O Holy heart,
This is my rendering of
your mild exhortations
to see with patience:

First,
      observe the greatest portion of this reflection.

First,
      observe the over–mind of nature
      that binds the race of mankind.

First,
      observe the light that blinds.

In this pawnshop of a universe
      things are arranged or exchanged not destroyed.

All the things on the shelf
      they know:
      this is a limited–time offer.

Know this
      instead of sorrow.

Believe It or Not

Half–truth, generality, paraphrase, innuendo, rumor, hearsay, heresy, best–
recollection, secondary source, speculation, word on the street, testimonial,
sources who decline to be named, exaggeration, sources whose identifying
information has been redacted for purposes the statement of which
has been redacted for reasons classified, statistical tendency, allegation,
guesswork, uncorroborated witness accounts

...all that: let's give it a name like "believe it or not."

Believe it or not, these are medicine:
snake oils, the application of leeches, worm pills, invigorators, elixirs,
electuaries, tinctures, pills, plasters, poultices, patent medicines,
aphrodisiacs.

Here are some colorful examples:
Lung Balm
Bromo–Seltzer
Burdock Blood Bitters
Boroleum Ointment
Dr. Burkhart's Vegetable Compound
Bateman's Pectoral Drops
Hooper's Female Pills
Carter's Little Liver Pills
Dr. Shoop's Restorative Nerve Pills
Sherman's Worm Lozenges

You are encouraged to try one of those but you should be advised that side
effects may include: headache (for which, incidentally, see above); severe
nausea, vomiting, or stomach pain; upset stomach, heartburn; drowsiness;
headache; fever lasting longer than 3 days; swelling; pain lasting longer
than 10 days; hearing problems; ringing in your ears; black, bloody, or tarry
stools; or coughing up blood or vomit that looks like coffee grounds.

Those are all things that might happen; they probably won't happen but they
might happen. To continue, these are some more things you can believe, or
not:

There is a global conspiracy to make people eat their vegetables; green M&M candies encourage sexual activity; the "Russian woodpecker" over–the–horizon radar signals heard on shortwave radio are actually a mind control experiment from which you can protect your brain by wearing tin–foil on your head or by wearing (insert non–headwear item here) on your head; the election at (insert time and place here) was rigged by (insert responsible party here); there's something sinister that they are not telling us about (insert historical event here).

Where "believe it or not" is concerned, you can (insert anything you like) in place of "it" because we believe that you are free to believe or to not believe whatever–the–hell–you–damn–well–please. We *could* not believe this. This hasn't always been a popular belief, but we believe this now, some of us, not all the time, still, we believe

but how are we to *know?*

How are we to be sure?

Be Sure

Be sure to think about your dreams and their meaning
Be sure to zip up your pants if you leave the house
Be sure to plan the seating arrangements carefully
Be sure to enjoy experiences you never would have
Be sure to go outdoors once in a while in winter
Be sure to take the keys before locking the car
Be sure to play the game at maximum difficulty
Be sure to check the potting soil for wetness
Be sure to expect a response within 48 hours
Be sure to watch for her celebrity comeback
Be sure to ask your waitress about dessert
Be sure to watch the thrilling conclusion
Be sure to have enough fuel for the trip
Be sure to wear proper safety equipment
Be sure to pack an extra pair of socks
Be sure to proofread your application
Be sure to wear flowers in your hair
Be sure to do objective fact–checks
Be sure to make reservations early
Be sure to watch the next episode
Be sure to request a window seat
Be sure to tie the knot tightly
Be sure to check the batteries
Be sure to take your medicine
Be sure to back up your data
Be sure to listen carefully
Be sure to get enough rest
Be sure to drink Ovaltine
Be sure to watch it live
Be sure to ride a train
Be sure to use muscles
Be sure to stand tall
Be sure to be social
Be sure to eat well
Be sure to lock up
Be sure to behave
Be sure to share
Be sure to vote
Be sure to see
Be sure to
Be sure

You Do Know, Don't You?

You do
Don't you?
You do know
Don't you?
You do know that
Don't you?
You do know I'm joking
Don't you?
You do know it's racist
Don't you?
You do know he's a fraud
Don't you?
You do know they are rich
Don't you?
You do know pride is a sin
Don't you?
You do know you're pregnant
Don't you?
You do know axed means fired
Don't you?
You do know that is expensive
Don't you?
You do know zombies aren't real
Don't you?
You do know patience is a virtue
Don't you?
You do know you sound very stupid
Don't you?
You do know women are human beings
Don't you?
You do know you're a complete wanker
Don't you?
You do know carcinogens cause disease
Don't you?
You do know how ridiculous that sounds
Don't you?
You do know you're begging the question
Don't you?
You do know the people on television can't hear you
Don't you?

A Live Studio Audience

You make us laugh
      Workplace situation comedy, you make us laugh
      Animated comedy, you make us laugh
      Ethnic situation comedy, you make us laugh
      Satirical news programs, you make us laugh
      Family situation comedy, you make us laugh
      Absurd comedy television, you make us laugh
      Sketch comedy television, you make us laugh
      Reality television comedy, you make us laugh
      Romantic situation comedy, you make us laugh
      Domestic situation comedy, you make us laugh
      Improvised situation comedy, you make us laugh

We laugh at your jokes
      Fat Albert, we laugh at your jokes
      I Dream of Jeannie, we laugh at your jokes
      Gilligan's Island, we laugh at your jokes
      Mister Ed, we laugh at your jokes
      Inspector Gadget, we laugh at your jokes
      Tonight Show, we laugh at your jokes
      Tonight Show Starring Johnny Carson, we laugh at your jokes
      Tonight Show with Jay Leno, we laugh at your jokes
      Tonight Show with Conan O'Brien, we laugh at your jokes
      Late Show, we laugh at your jokes
      The Late Late Show, we laugh at your jokes

You make us laugh
    You make us laugh
    You make us laugh
    You make us laugh

We laugh at your jokes
    We laugh at your jokes
    We laugh at your jokes
    We laugh at your jokes

We laugh
    We laugh
    We laugh
    We laugh

Four Years Closer

We're four years closer to the day when our enemies will have the bomb. We're
four years closer to the end of the world. We're four years further away
from the beginning of the world than we were four years ago. We're four
years closer to the day the sun will exhaust its fuel, speaking of atomic
energy, and on that day, a day we're now four years closer to, on that day
the sun will swallow the earth. We're also four years closer to a sustainable
future. We're four years closer to my fortieth birthday, my forty–fourth
birthday, and four years closer to the day that I will die. We're four years
further away from the day I slipped and fell on the playground and skinned
up my leg. Four years later, there was a scar there. Many years later, I can't
see that scar anymore. We're four years closer to the year 2052. We're four
years closer to flying cars, to men on mars, drinkless bars, harvesting the
stars, artificially intelligent avatars, the war to end all wars. We're four
years closer to the largest population ever recorded on Earth. We're four
years closer to a larger national debt, not the deficit, the debt. We're four
years closer to the last time you'll ever eat ice cream. We're four years
closer to the death of the oldest tree in the city of Baltimore. We're four
years closer to the extinction of another species. We're four years closer to
the exhaustion of all the petroleum, all the iron, the wood, water, copper,
tin, nickel, sulphur, diamonds, emeralds, rubies, laughter, clay, oxygen, ice,
snowball fights, elbow room, landscapes without billboards, sandalwood
extract, cork, blue corn and all the other shit we'll have less of in four years.
We're four years closer to retirement.

We're four years closer to paying our student loans, our medical bills, our
mortgages, our credit card bills, our car payments, our insurance, but in
for years we'll still be paying for cable, internet, cell phone data plans,
gasoline, insurance payments, taxes, taxes, taxes. We can't tax or save our
way out of this one. Time to pony up! Maybe in four years we'll pony up.
We're four years closer to four years from now when we'll pony up. We'll
pony up then. Pick another date we're four years closer to. We're ten years
closer, too. We're twenty years closer. Those of us who have been on this
rock long enough are fifty, sixty maybe even seventy years closer to that
date. We're ten thousand years closer to ten thousand years from now than
we were ten thousand years ago. We're four years closer to being further
from the beginning.

Every day begins a period that will end in a thousand years, just as each day is
the end of an age that began that long ago. Why make distinctions? Time is
not against us; it is only our perception of its end that fills us with dread.

Love Is on the Radio

Love is beginning now
Love is barely dressed
Love is a bit out of phase
Love is a mind confused
Love is a rose but you better not pick it
Love is a mystery
Love is actually helping or hindering
Love is stronger than pride
Love is only for the lucky and the strong
Love is a twelve–bar blues
Love is your love
Love is the light of the world
Love is an open door
Love is a heart abused
Love is lost, and lost is love
Love is all you need
Love is a mine of gold
Love is its own reward
Love is my drug
Love is a morning song
Love is dangerous
Love is it can make you laugh
Love is I want you to show me
Love is like a red, red rose
Love is tragedy
Love is blindness
Love is like oxygen
Love is your blue suede shoes
Love is a steel guitar
Love is on the way
Love is a river
Love is a red dress well hang me in rags
Love is a drowning soul
Love is enough to light up the darkness

Love is a miracle
Love is here with me
Love is watching you go
Love is one way no way
Love is king
Love is calling
Love is beautiful
Love is a losing game
Love is a battle scar
Love is a many–splendored thing
Love is stronger than justice
Love is still a band of gold
Love is a bourgeois construct
Love is made of something
Love is the pleasures I'm told
Love is relentless
Love is a shiny car
Love is like an antidote
Love is misplaced

Easier Said Than Done

The total conversion of matter into energy is theoretically possible by throwing
matter into a black hole, thus consuming the matter and emitting heat,
which could be used to generate power.

Easier said than done.

That two bodies should occupy the same place, that the sun should recede
or stand still, something that nature can do, but not in the same order,
something that nature cannot do.

Easier said than done.

The holy man was put to death for his holiness, death by beheading, martyred.
Death in an instant. A profusion of blood. A woman wept and kept some
blood in a vial, held carefully, ages through ages, blood to dust.

Dust to blood. Dust to blood!

The vial is presented to the gathered mass and held aloft for all to see, full
of dust, but with time, patience and belief, the dust becomes blood.
Liquefaction and rejoicing. The dust is blood.

Easier said than done.

The void colony of Roanoke left its houses. The cries of the baby girl could not
be heard. Management had been delayed by other significant priorities.
A carving, on a tree, of the name of an island. The cries of the baby girl
could not be heard. Management set out to travel to that island, during a
hurricane.

Easier said than done.

A golden city at the heart of a golden kingdom at the heart of a golden empire,
ruled by a king, adorned in gold, riding the wind across the lake, in a
golden raft laden with gold, bearing gold offerings to the golden god of
the lake. The gold sinks, slowly, down, below the surface of the water,
beyond the light of the sun. Gold is not gold in the darkness. It sinks into the
darkness inhabited by the god of gold in the darkness, to the city there in
that lake, the city of El Dorado. The city is marked on a map. The map is the
guide. The map is published and easy to read. Famous men and noble men
have read the map. The map clearly indicates the location of the City of El
Dorado, the source of all that gold.

Easier said than done.

I'm Sorry It's Been a While but You Know How It Is...

When you're too busy being happy
tying ties and shoelaces
waiting in line at the pharmacy

When you're too busy being happy
wondering whether there will be parking available
having the perennial argument but not argument about what's for dinner
sorting the junk mail from the good stuff

When you're too busy being happy
defrosting the freezer
adjusting the thermostat

When you're too busy being happy
buying things on sale
smelling the milk in the middle of the night for signs of its age
looking for the remote

When you're too busy being happy
executing commands like:
select, copy, paste, select, cut, undo

When you're too busy being happy
cleaning out old boxes in the closet
wondering whether today's interest rate is a better interest rate
removing the dust that collects

When you're too busy being happy
brushing twice and flossing
pairing the socks

When you're too busy being happy
blocking out life for work
blocking out work for life
answering the phone, sometimes

When you're too busy being happy
using television to look at the sky
arriving simultaneously at a four-way stop

Notes

Believe It or Not
The list of 19th Century patent medicines was sampled from a catalogue of the Smithsonian's collection. As with many of these poems, the key phrase is a commonplace one.

Be Sure
These lines are a mixture of found examples, paraphrases, and imagined examples of the phrase.

You Do Know, Don't You?
These lines are sampled from real conversations.

Love Is on the Radio
The phrase "love is" occurs frequently in the lyrics of popular songs. These lines are all examples from an inexhaustible supply.

Easier Said than Done
In some religious settings, a litany is a text or incantation with two parts: "versus," recited by one person and the "responsum," intoned by the people gathered. This piece has a similar structure.

Made in the USA
San Bernardino, CA
23 June 2015